30-AGO-161

Alaska is a state with breathtaking scenery,
wild animals, and an interesting history full
of adventure and gold rushes.
This pretty picture book will take you to some
of Alaska's most beautiful places and will
introduce you to some of its biggest treasures.
Enjoy!

Acknowledgements:
We are grateful to the following for repeatedly assisting us with our book projects:
Bob & Pam Gilbertson, Ingo Richter, Lynne Beykirch, Pam "the Grammar Cop" Patterson,
Scott & Kasey Goss, Cindy & Wray Kinard, Dean Philips, and our editor, Linda Thurston.

To our parents and grandparents who never had the opportunity to visit this great land of Alaska.

Text and illustration copyright © 2006 by Bernd and Susan Richter
Printed in China; First Printing, February 2007
ISBN # 1-931353-36-0

Designed, produced, published, and distributed in Alaska by:
    Bernd and Susan Richter
    Saddle Pal Creations, Inc., P.O. Box 872127, Wasilla, Ak 99687, USA
All rights reserved. No portion of this book may be reproduced in any
form without the publisher's written approval.

More children's books by Bernd and Susan Richter available
from Saddle Pal Creations, Inc.:

* When Grandma and Grandpa Visited Alaska They ...
* Grandma and Grandpa Cruise Alaska's Inside Passage
* Grandma and Grandpa Visit Denali National Park
* Grandma and Grandpa Ride the Alaska Train
* Alaska Animals - Where Do They Go at 40 Below?
* Touch and Feel Alaska's Animals (board book)
* Uncover Alaska's Wonders (a lift-the-flap book)
* The Little Bear Who Didn't Want to Hibernate
* The Twelve Days of Christmas in Alaska
* Goodnight Alaska - Goodnight Little Bear (board book)
* Peek-A-Boo Alaska (lift-the-flap board book)
* How Animal Moms Love Their Babies (board book)
* When Grandma and Grandpa cruised through AK (board book)

* How Alaska Got Its Flag (with flag song CD)
* Discover Alaska's Denali Park
* Do Alaskans Live in Igloos?
* Cruising Alaska's Inside Passage
* Listen to Alaska's Animals (sound book)
* She's My Mommy Too!
* When Grandma visited Alaska she ...
* Alaskan Toys for Girls and Boys
* My Alaska Animals - Can You Name Them?
* A Bus Ride Into Denali (board book)
* Grandma and Grandpa Love Their RV
* Old Maid - Alaska Style (card game)
   .... and more

Look at these books by visiting our website **www.alaskachildrensbooks.com**

Traveling Alaska

A Children's Book
by
Bernd and Susan Richter

Published by
Saddle Pal Creations, Inc., Wasilla, Alaska, USA

Do you know what and where Alaska is?

Alaska, shown in dark blue on this map, is the largest and northernmost state of the 50 states that make up the United States of America. It is separated from the 48 contiguous states by the country called Canada and from the 50th state, Hawaii, by the Pacific Ocean.

You can tell from this map that Alaska may be very far away from where you live.
Since Alaska is so far away, how do you think we got there?

Alaska (USA)

Canada

48 contiguous United States

Hawaii (USA)

The fastest way to get to Alaska is by airplane. Can you guess how long such a flight would take from where you live? Let me give you a hint. From anywhere in the USA, a flight to Alaska will take from a few hours to a whole day. People who live outside North America may have to fly for more than 24 hours to visit Alaska.

Have you ever flown? If so, did you like it?

In Alaska, the three major cities, Anchorage, Juneau and Fairbanks, are where most of the big airplanes land. The biggest city, Anchorage, is located between tall mountains and the ocean as shown in this picture.

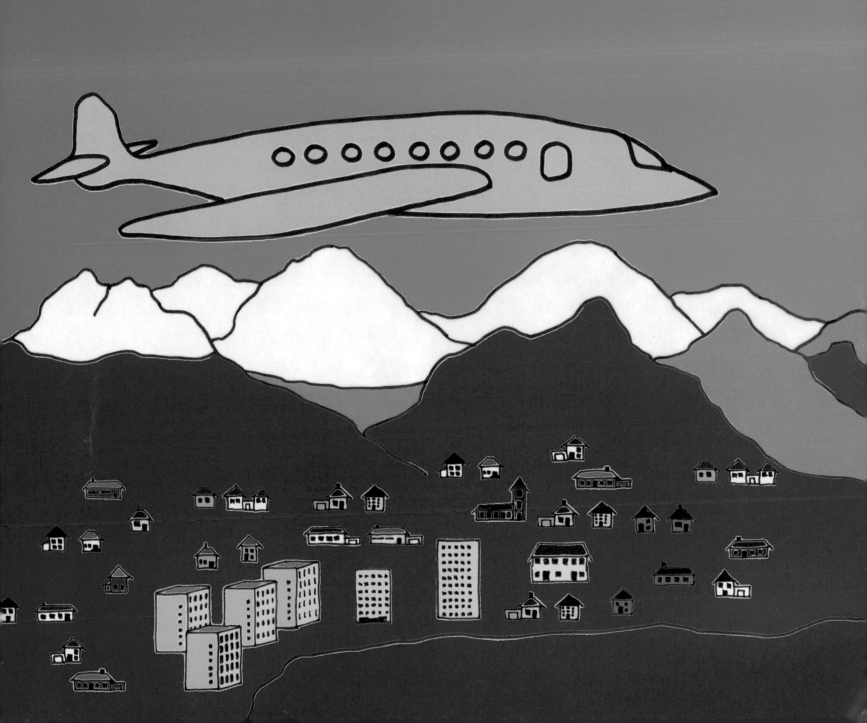

Another way to travel to Alaska is by ship but it takes longer to get there. Every summer, cruise ships sail north to bring hundreds of thousands of visitors to this enchanting land. Do you know what cruise ships are? They are big ships with room for hundreds or even thousands of passengers. Because it takes cruise ships several days to get to Alaska, they are like floating hotels. They have bedrooms, dining rooms, and shops on board. The biggest ships even have swimming pools and basketball courts. When people want to take their cars with them on a ship to Alaska, they take ships called ferries.

Have you been on a cruise ship or a ferry? If so, you have to tell me about your boating adventures.

CRUISE SHIP

From the ship, passengers see the coast and the tall mountains of Alaska. Some of these mountains are so high that the snow on them never melts. As the snow gets thicker with each winter, glaciers are formed. Glaciers are like rivers made of snow and ice. Just like rivers, they flow from high elevations to low elevations, only much, much slower. In fact, they move so slowly that one can't tell that they are moving except when pieces of ice break off at the very front of it. When pieces fall off into water they are called icebergs.

What do you think happens to icebergs in the water? Will they float, will they sink to the bottom, or will they melt? Find out when you take your next bath. Ask your mom or dad to put some ice cubes into your bath water. Then watch what happens to the ice.

People on the ships like to watch animals that live in the ocean. Can you name any animals that live in the ocean?

Have you ever heard of sea otters? In Alaska, everybody loves watching sea otter families because otters are so cute and playful, just like little children. Otters often swim right next to the ships, eating crabs and clams. They do that while floating on their backs. Floating is easy for them because they have thick fur that traps air and works just like an air mattress.

Many whales live in the waters off the coast of Alaska. Sometimes whales can be seen swimming at the ocean surface. The tops of their heads show during breathing, and their tails pop up just as they dive again. When they are having lots of fun playing, they sometimes jump all the way out of the water.

Do you know how large a whale can get? The bigger ones are as long as a semi truck with a trailer! That's big!

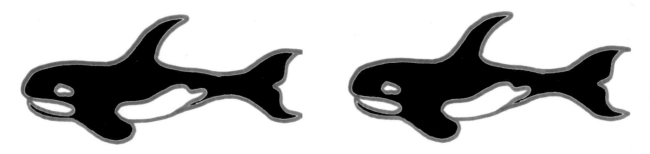

14

Many birds live along the coast. Some of them are the same kinds of birds that live in your backyard. Others live in faraway places, such as Alaska. One of these is the puffin, shown in this picture. With its yellow and red beak and with its orange legs and feet, it can be seen from far away. Have you ever seen such a funny looking bird? Of course, they aren't funny if you are a fish!

Are there any similar birds where you live? Can you name birds that live in your backyard?

The ships stop at villages and towns along the coast to let passengers go shopping or sightseeing. And there is lots to see and plenty to do!

Just look at this interesting house with totem poles. Do you know where totem poles come from? Totem poles are carved by Native people of Alaska out of very tall trees. The carvings show faces of people and of different animals, such as frogs, birds, and fish. These faces and animals tell family stories just like this picture book tells a story.

Can you find any frogs on these totem poles? What else can you find?

18

Since Alaska is a very big state, many visitors take a train to see more of the land. The train runs from the coast to the Interior. On the way, passengers see huge mountain ranges, including Mt. McKinley, North America's highest mountain, and large forests, big rivers, and sometimes even wild animals.

Do you like trains? Have you ever been on one?

If you haven't, you should try it one day. It will be fun!

The train stops at Denali National Park where many wild animals live. This park is like a HUGE zoo but without fences. All the animals, even the big grizzly bears, can wander around wherever they want to while looking for something to eat or for a place to sleep. They find their own food and take care of themselves. People are not allowed to feed the animals here as they do in most zoos. These wild animals remain free in their wilderness home in Denali Park. People are guests who can visit the animals there and then go back home.

Can you find in this picture some of the wild animals that live in the park? Can you identify the bear, the wolf, the caribou and the moose?

22

Denali National Park

Did you find the moose? If not, here's one closer up. Have you ever seen a moose before? Are there moose where you live?

Moose are usually even bigger than horses. Male moose can be recognized easily by their big antlers which grow on their heads each year. Can you think of other animals with antlers? Or how about animals with horns?

What kind of food do you think a moose likes to eat? Often, one can see moose feeding in small ponds or lakes. Could they be eating fish? NO! Moose love to eat the juicy grasses that grow on the bottom of lakes. But they also like leaves from alder bushes. And in the winter, when ponds are frozen and leaves have fallen, they eat the tender branches off bushes and trees.

Whoa, what do we have here? Have you ever seen a bear? Not a teddy bear but a REAL bear?

One place to see bears is in a zoo. There they are kept in cages or behind big walls because bears can be very dangerous. In Alaska, bears still live in the wild. In the spring, one can see bear moms with their cubs that were born during last winter and now like to play in the meadows after all the snow has melted. Mama bear watches out so that nobody comes too close to her cubs. That's why it is important for visitors to stay far away and hidden when watching bears and other wild animal moms with babies. I love watching wild animals but I am careful never to get too close to them. You should be too!

Where the trains and ships can't go, visitors can travel by automobile on Alaska's roads. Some people drive their own cars to Alaska, others rent one. Many use recreational vehicles, just like this one. Recreational vehicles are great for travel because they have a kitchen, beds, and usually a bathroom.

Have you ever been in such a recreational vehicle? Do you think you would rather sleep in one of them or in a tent? How about when it rains? Where would you rather be then?

 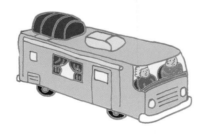 

28

Many people come to Alaska because there are lots of big fish in its rivers. Every summer, hundreds of thousands of fish called salmon swim from the ocean up the rivers to the places where they were born a few years earlier. This is called a salmon run. When that happens, people rush to the rivers to either watch the run or catch the fish.

Do you like eating fish? These fish taste very good!

30

Not everybody goes to the rivers for the fish. Instead, some go there to search for gold which can be found in the ground along many creeks and rivers in Alaska. Do you know what gold is? Can you name something that is made from gold?

Looking for gold is hard work. At the river, this miner first digs holes in the ground with a shovel. He then puts everything he dug up into a gold pan. Finally, he washes the gravel, sand, and mud out of the gold pan into the river. If he is lucky, there will be gold left in the pan after all the hard work. This miner is happy because he found some big gold nuggets. But not everybody is this lucky.

Can you imagine a place where it doesn't get dark at night?

9 P.M.

Midnight

3 A.M

Well, Alaska is such a place during the summer. It doesn't get dark because the sun goes down very late at night and rises again soon after in the morning. In fact, in northernmost Alaska, the sun doesn't set at all for two months in the middle of the summer! Then children play outside when it's already dark where you live and people go to sleep when it's still light outside. Would you like that? Do you think you could sleep if it wouldn't get dark in your room?

34

Backwoods
Lodge

Just the opposite happens in the winter. In northern Alaska in the middle of the winter, the sun never comes up in the morning at all and it stays dark all day. In fact, along the northern coast of Alaska, it is dark for two months in a row! This is a great time to see the northern lights. Do you know what northern lights are? They are bright bands of light, mostly gray, but sometimes pink, red, or green. They swirl around the sky as if someone had turned on a huge multicolored flashlight and pointed it at the dark sky. When the lights are visable starting in late summer, people go outside to watch them just like people watch fireworks on the 4th of July or at New Year's.

Can you see the northern lights where you live?

Along the northern coast of Alaska nearest to the North Pole, it is so cold that the entire ocean is filled with ice and icebergs for most of the year. This is where Alaska's largest land animal, the polar bear, lives. Polar bears are magnificent animals with coats as white as snow. They are dangerous to be around, but not many people live where polar bears are. That's why most people go to the zoo to see polar bears. Have you been to a zoo and have you seen a polar bear there? If you haven't been to a zoo, you should go one day. There will be animals from all over the world!

At a time almost as long ago as when
the dinosaurs lived, an animal even
bigger than the polar bear --
the woolly mammoth -- made its
home in Alaska. The woolly mammoth looked a lot like
an elephant except that it had very long fur to protect
it from the cold. Today, there are no live mammoths
left in Alaska, so we can't see them in the wild. But
maybe one of your ancient relatives saw them a long
time ago while visiting Alaska. Can you find the people
in this picture who might have been your old relatives?

Once in a while, the bones of mammoths are found by
people digging in the earth. These bones are then
brought to museums for display. Have you been to such
a museum? There are usually a lot of neat things to
do and to see.

40

This is the end of our travels through beautiful Alaska. We certainly had lots of fun and learned a lot, didn't we? And there is so much more to see in Alaska and the world. A few years from now when you are grown up, perhaps you will travel to Alaska yourself. Maybe you will remember all the pictures and stories from this book.

With much love from,

....

Fairbanks

Mt. McKinley

Denali Natl. Park

Anchorage

Juneau

Good-bye Alaska

Your Travel Log Here

——— **Your Photos Here** ———

Your Travel Log Here

Your Photos Here

Your Travel Log Here